Take some cheery words,
add a few kind thoughts,
and as you'll soon see
these are meant to be
honey from my heart.

Honey from My Heart for You, Mother

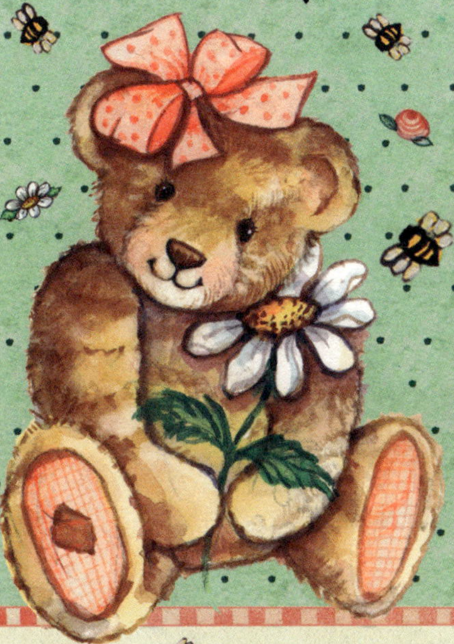

Illustrated by Debra Jordan Bryan

Copyright of
illustrations © 2002
by Debra Jordan Bryan

Published by J Countryman
A division of Thomas Nelson, Inc.,
Nashville, Tennessee 37214

Project Editor—Terri Gibbs

All rights reserved. No portion of this publication may be reproduced, stored in a retrieval system or transmitted in any form by any means—electronic, mechanical, photocopying, recording, or any other—except for brief quotations in printed reviews, without the prior written permission of the publisher.

Designed by Left Coast Design, Portland, OR

ISBN: 0-8499-9533-7

www.jcountryman.com
www.thomasnelson.com

Printed in China

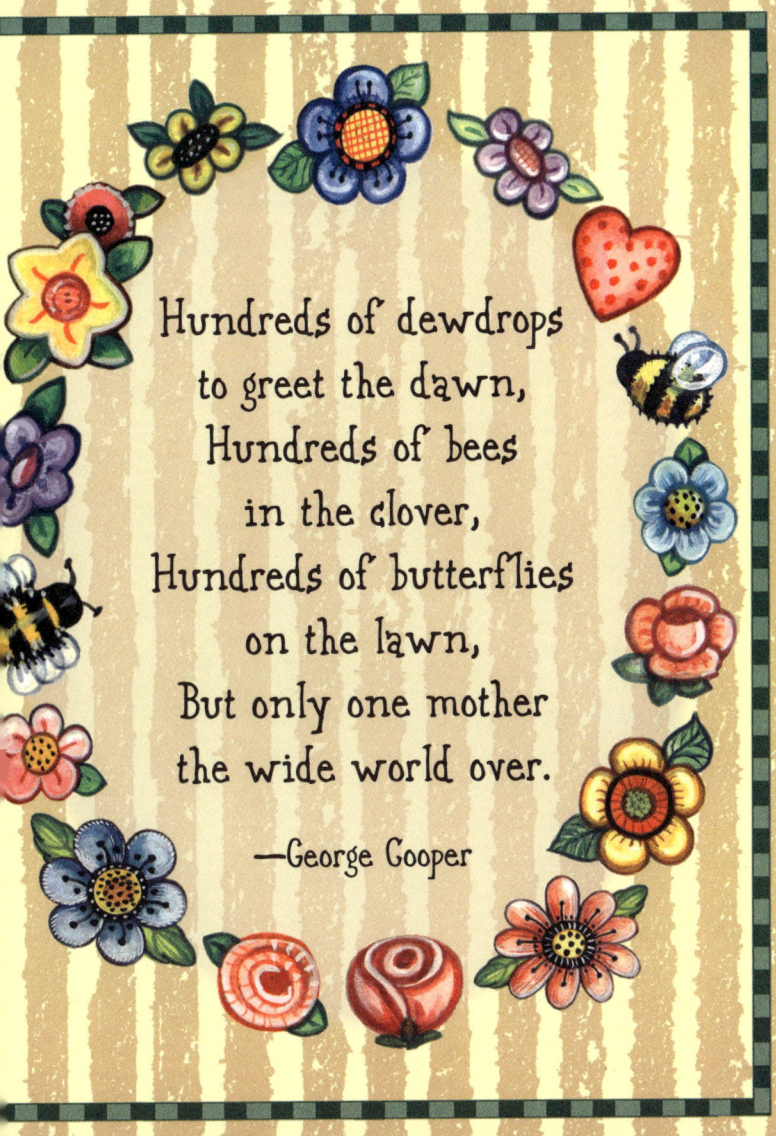

God gives us friends—
and that means much;
but far above all others,
the greatest of His gifts
was when He thought
of mothers.

—Anonymous

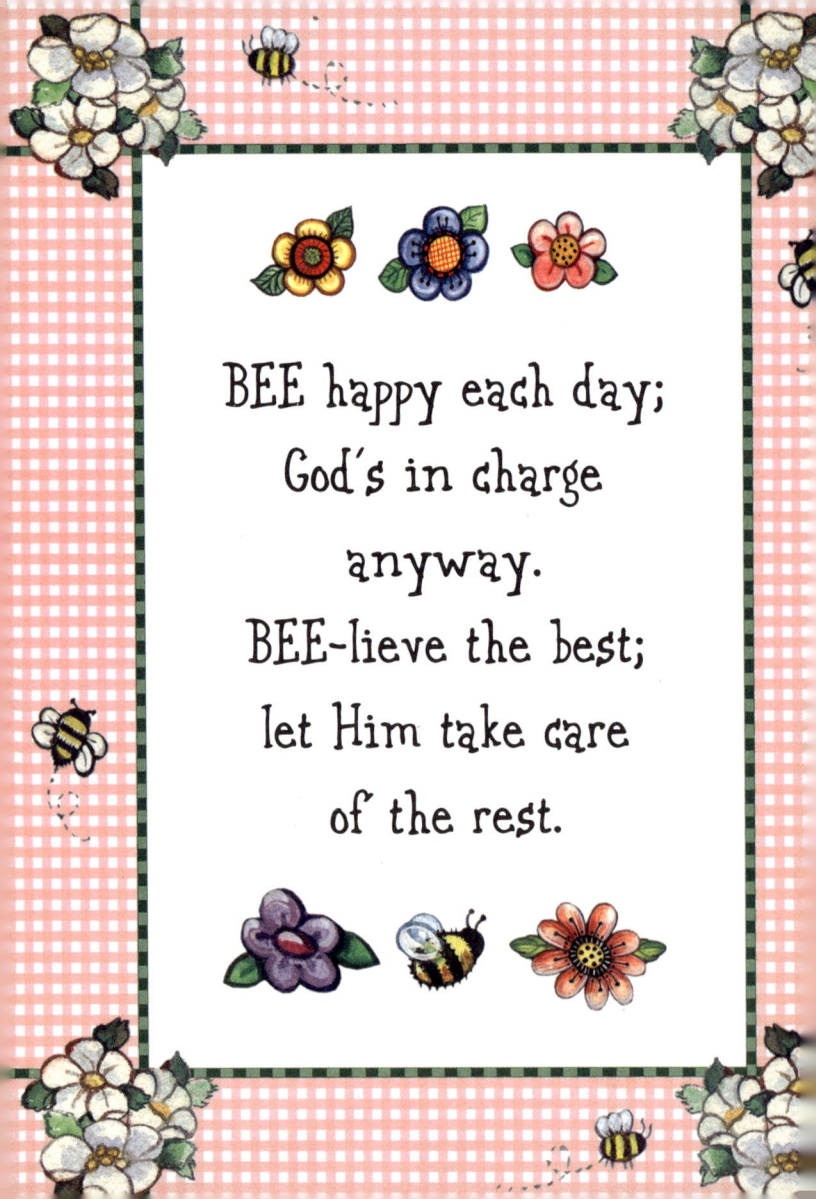

A little prayer for you Mom: